ENGRAVED FLOWERS

Coloring Book

By Brittany Skye

ISBN-13: 978-1517008703
ISBN-10: 1517008700

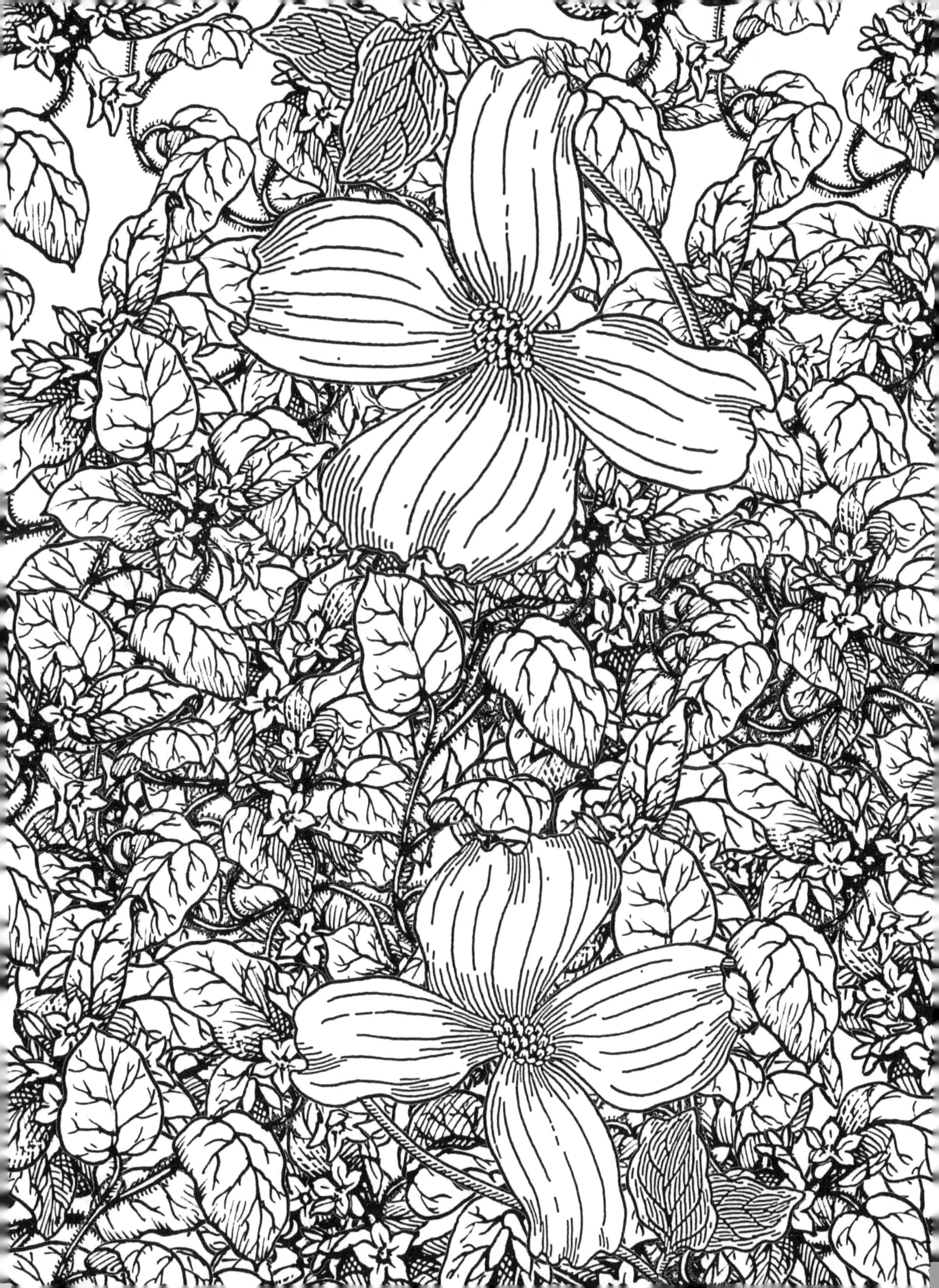

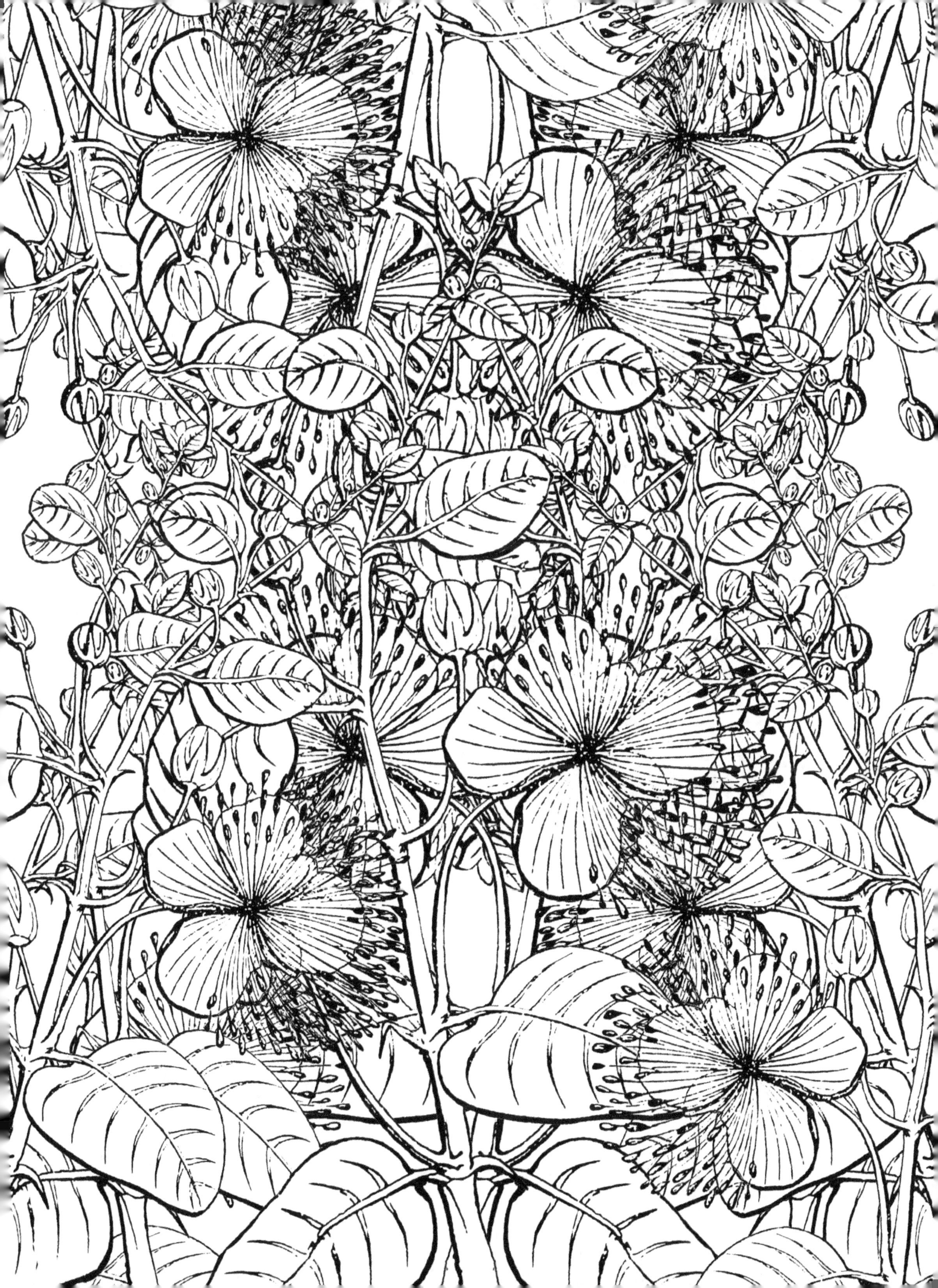

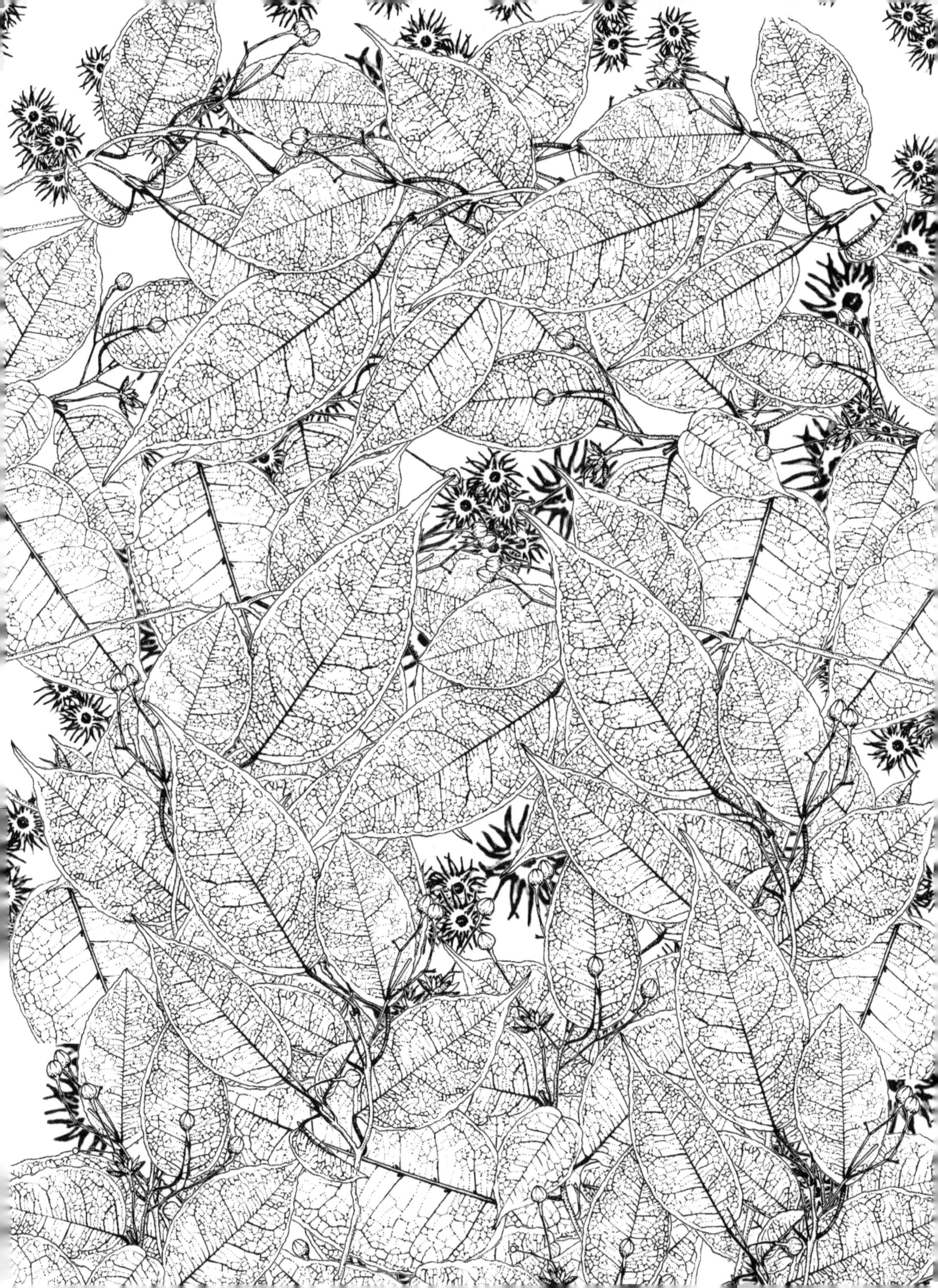

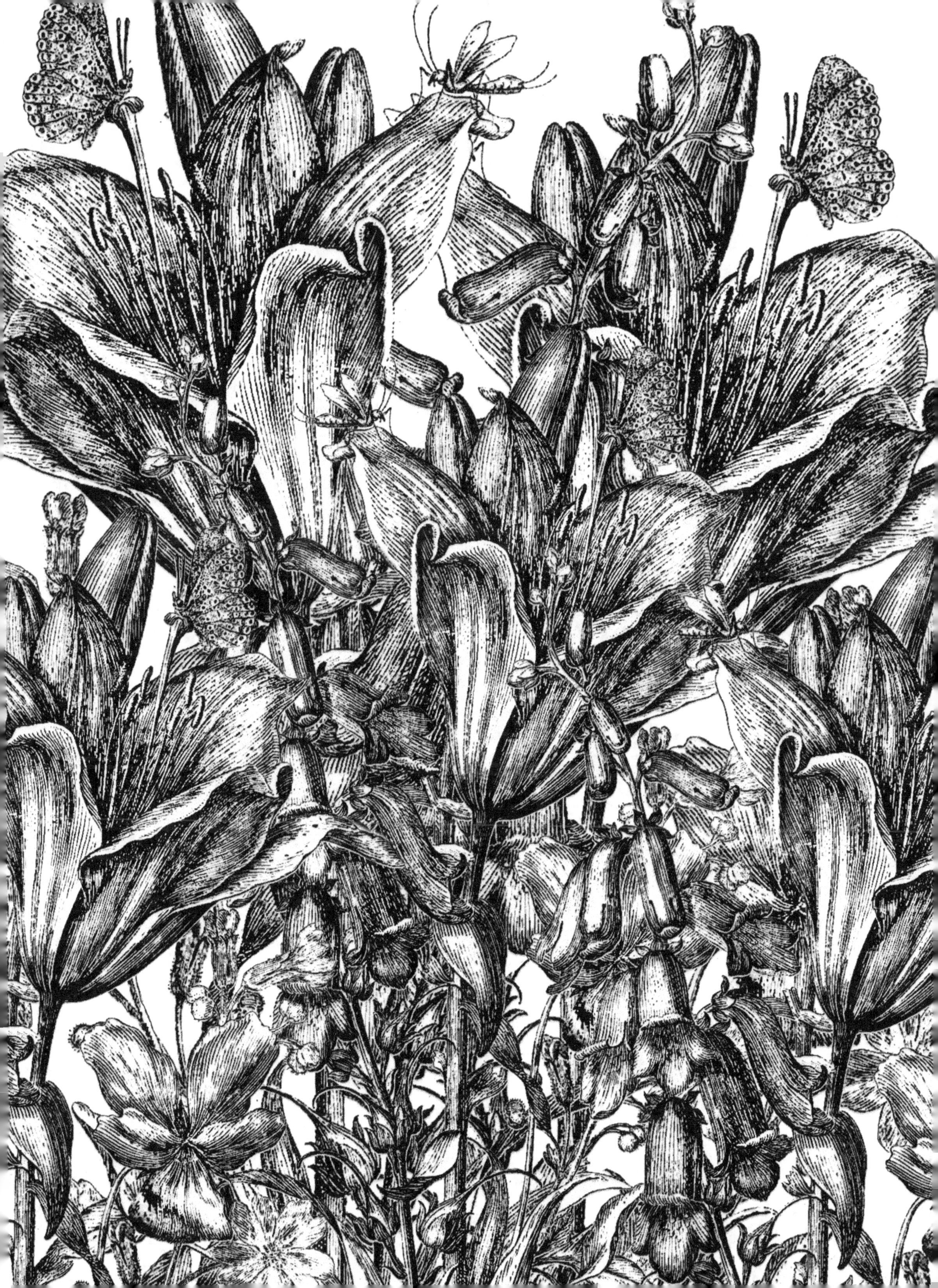

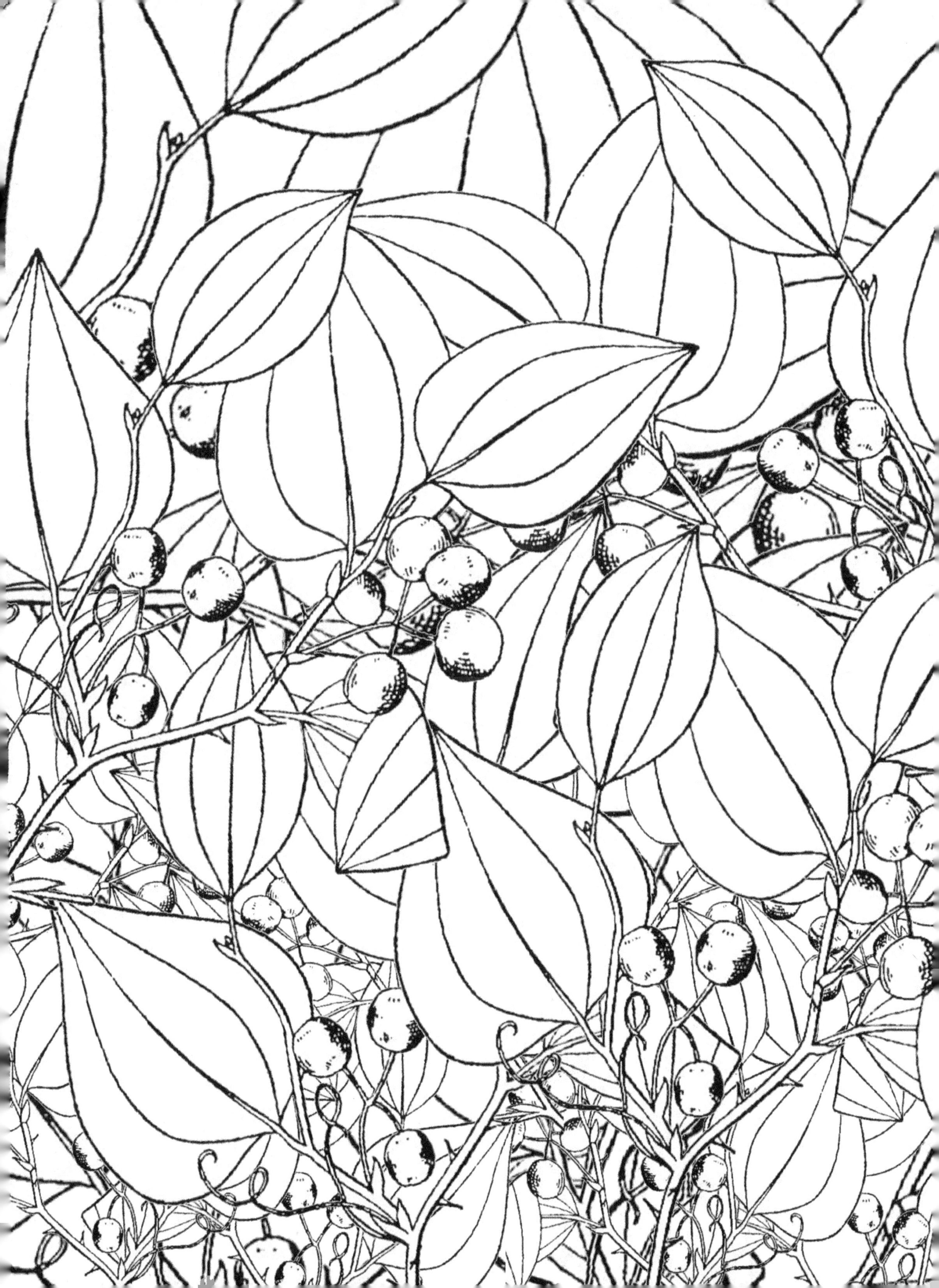

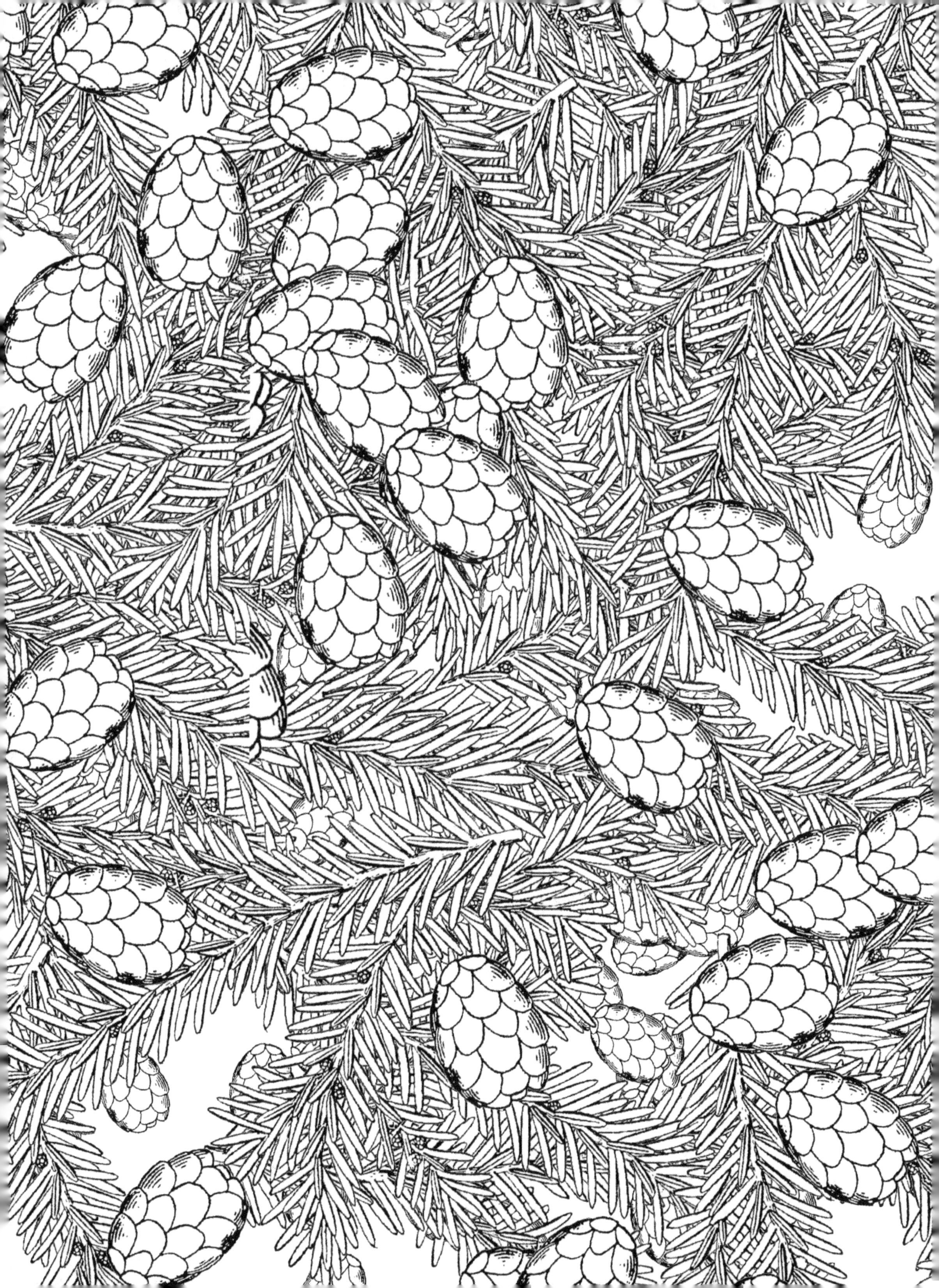

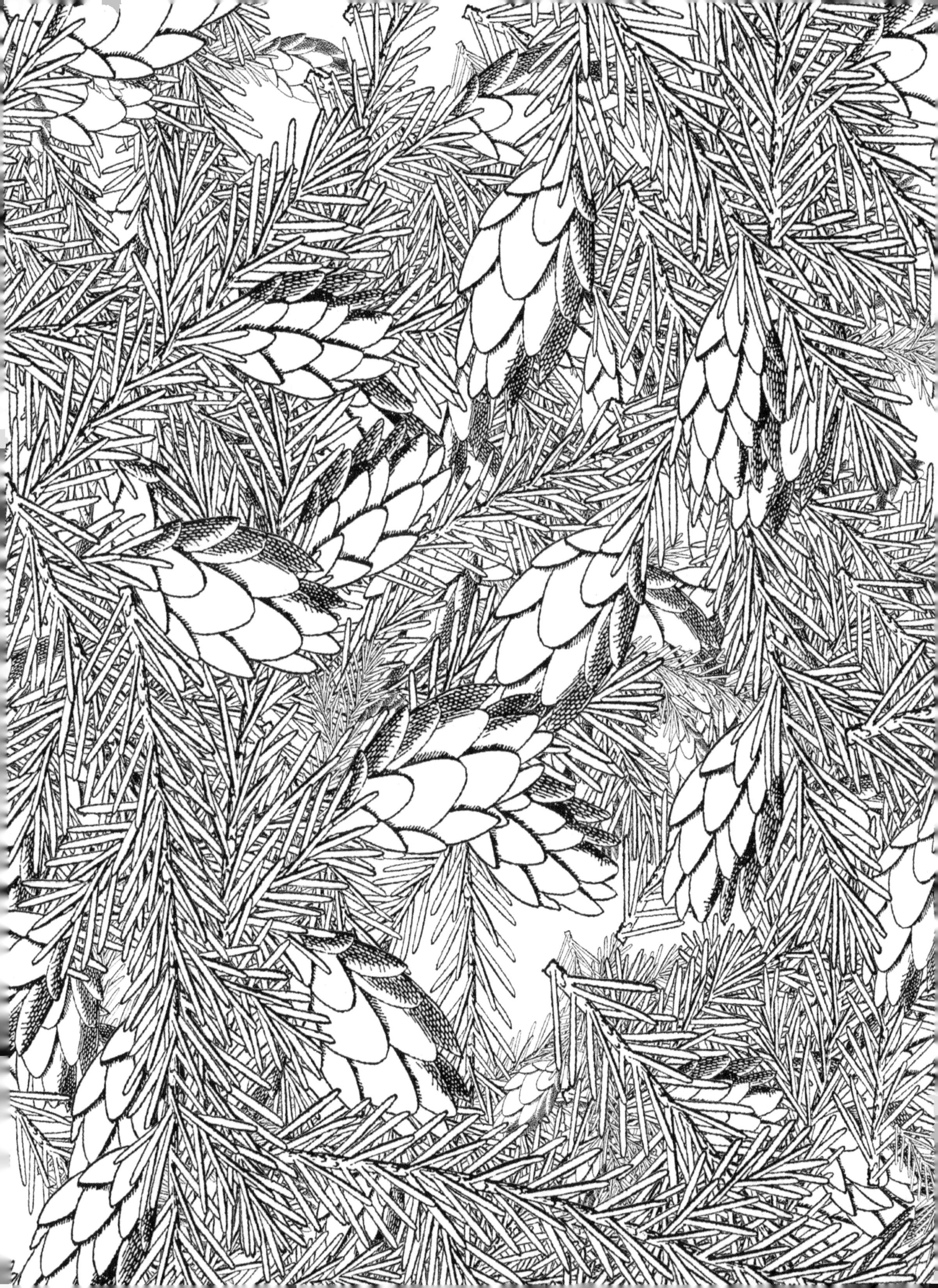

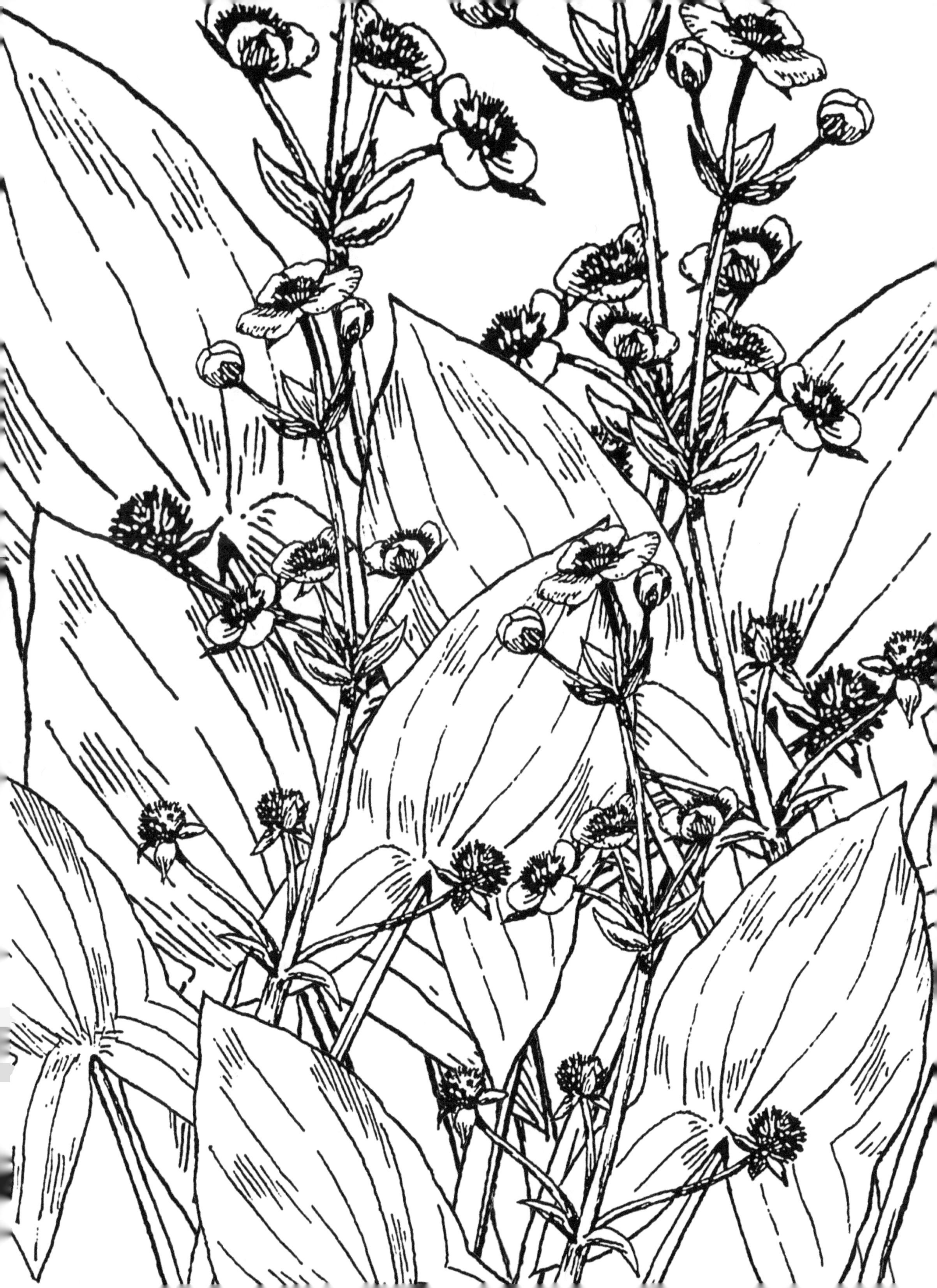

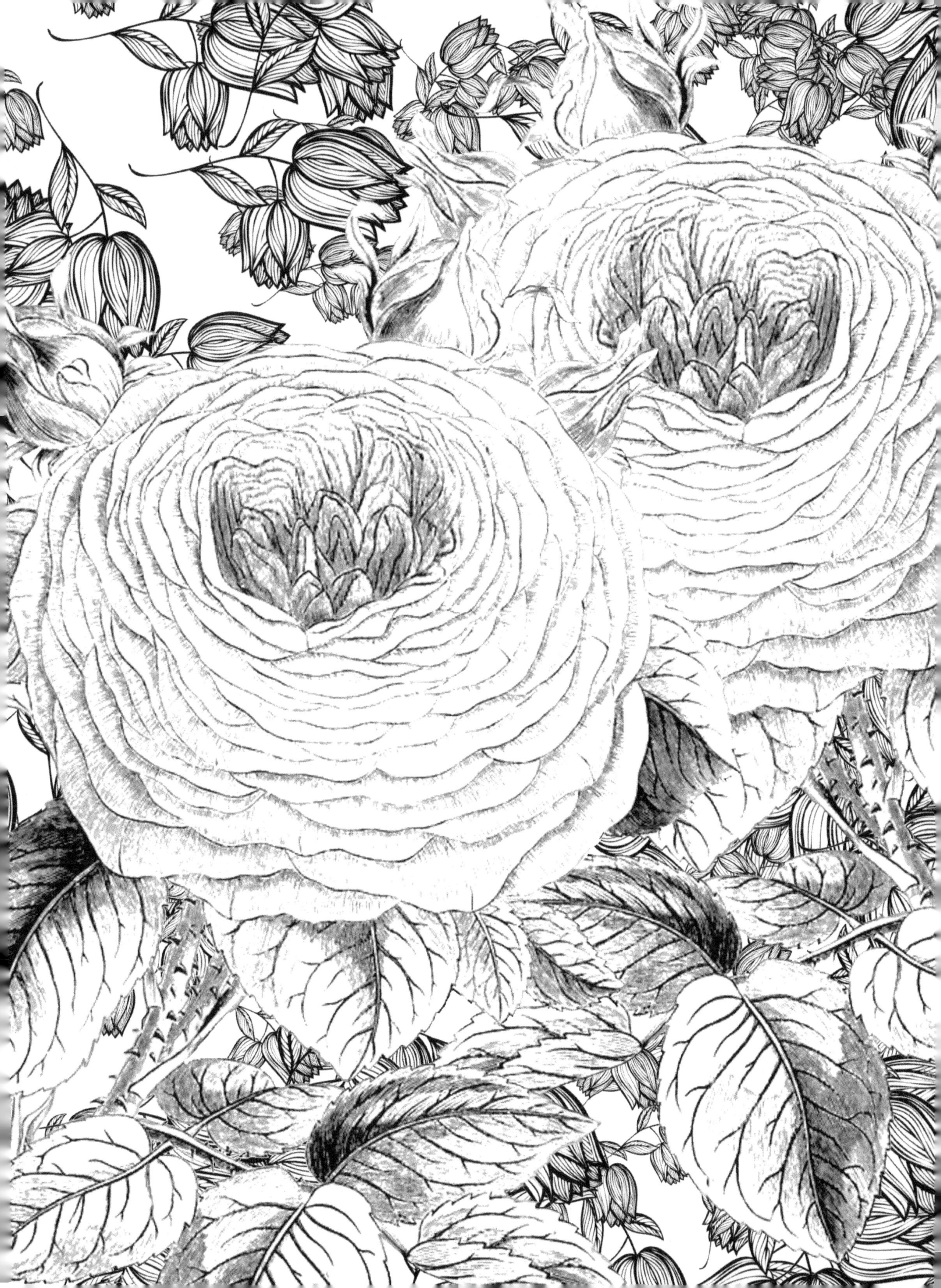

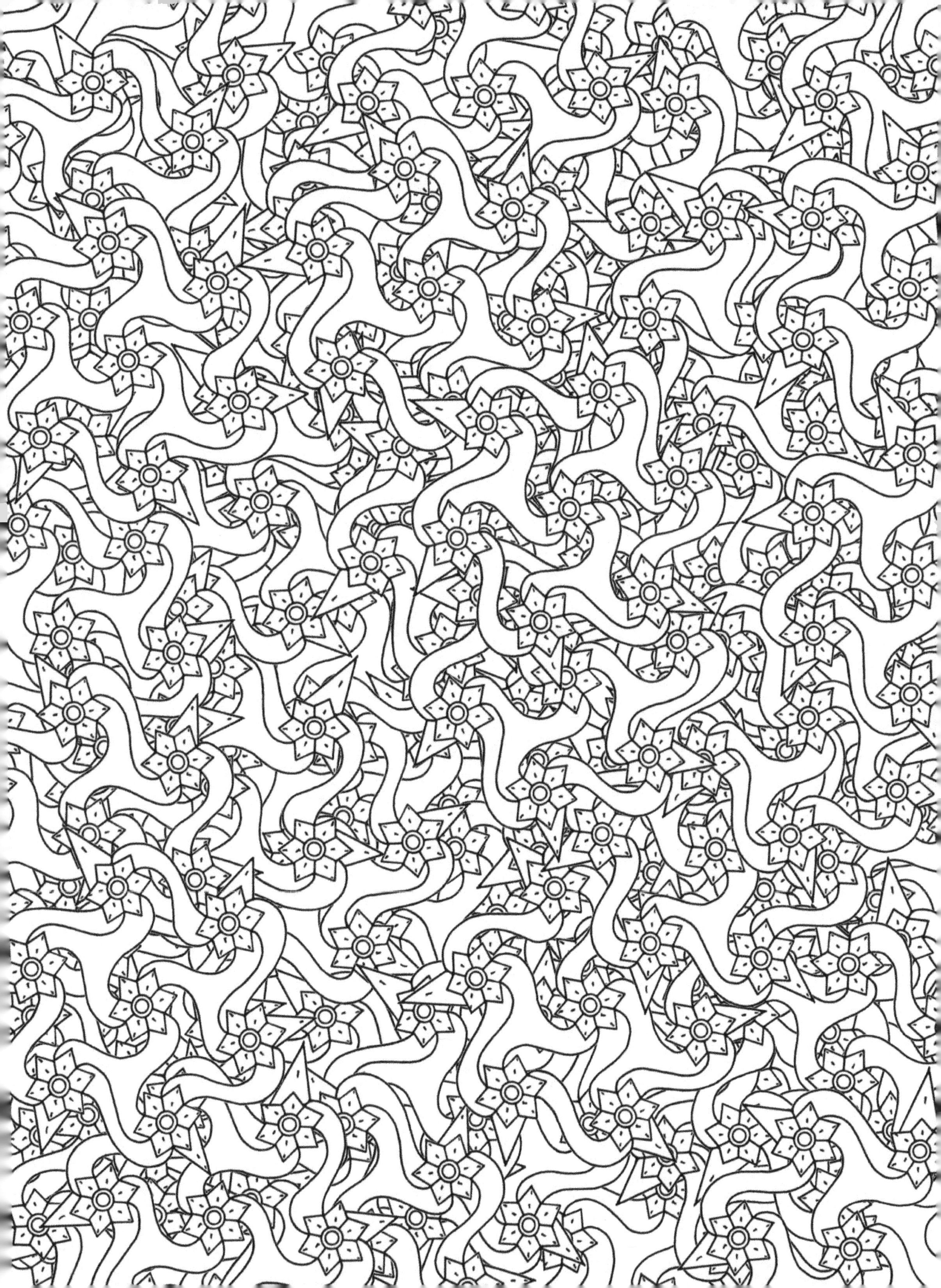

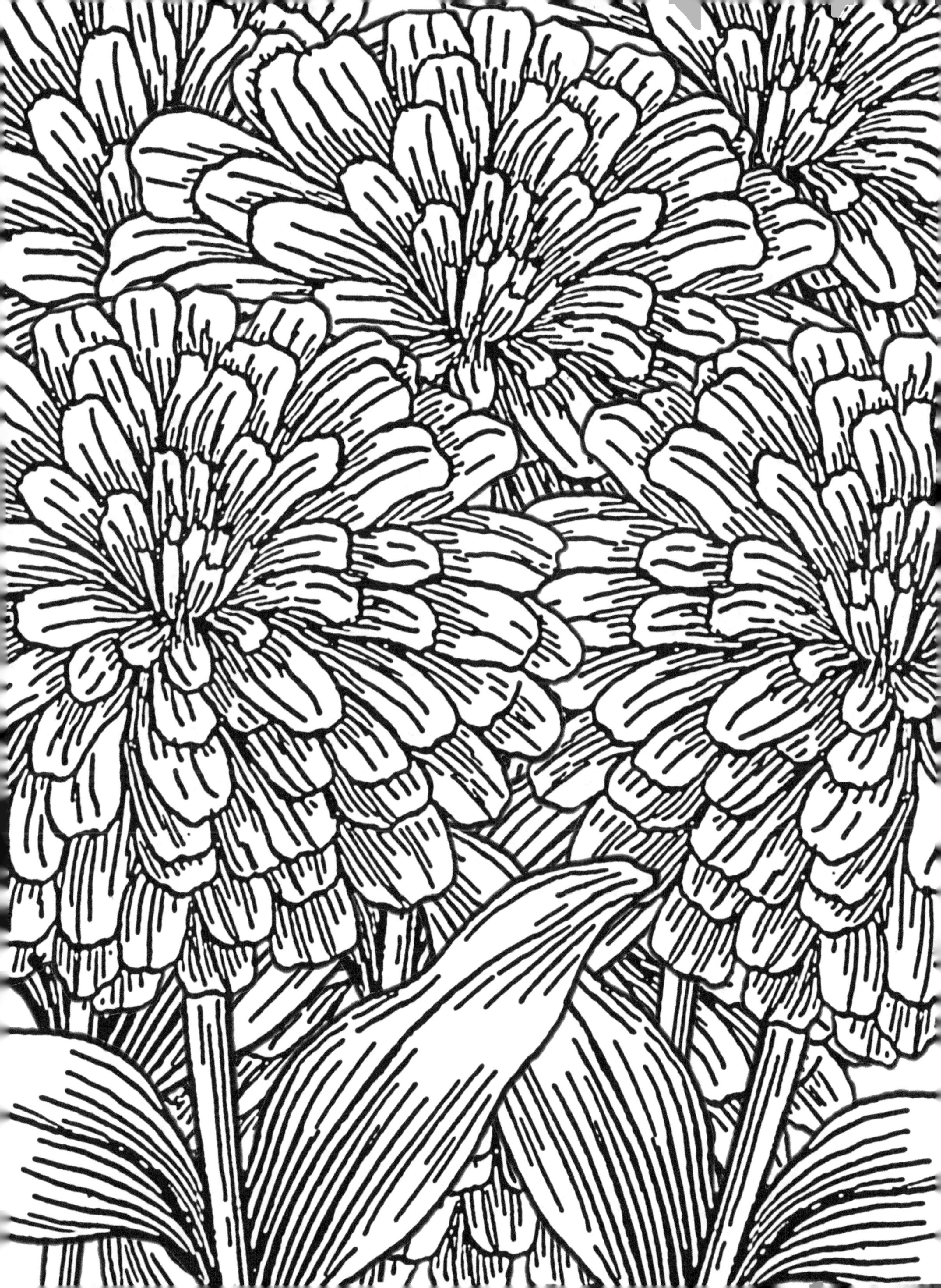

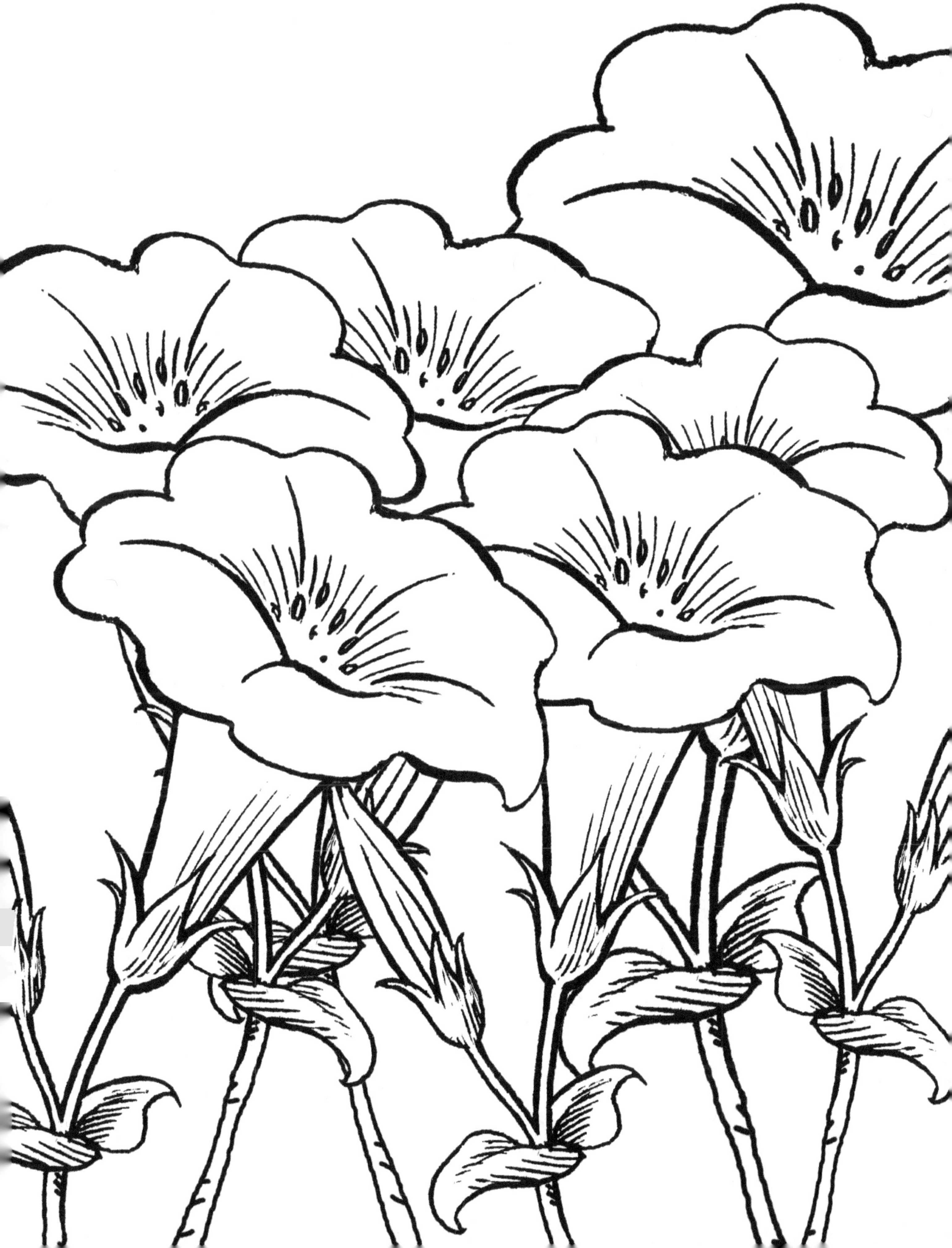

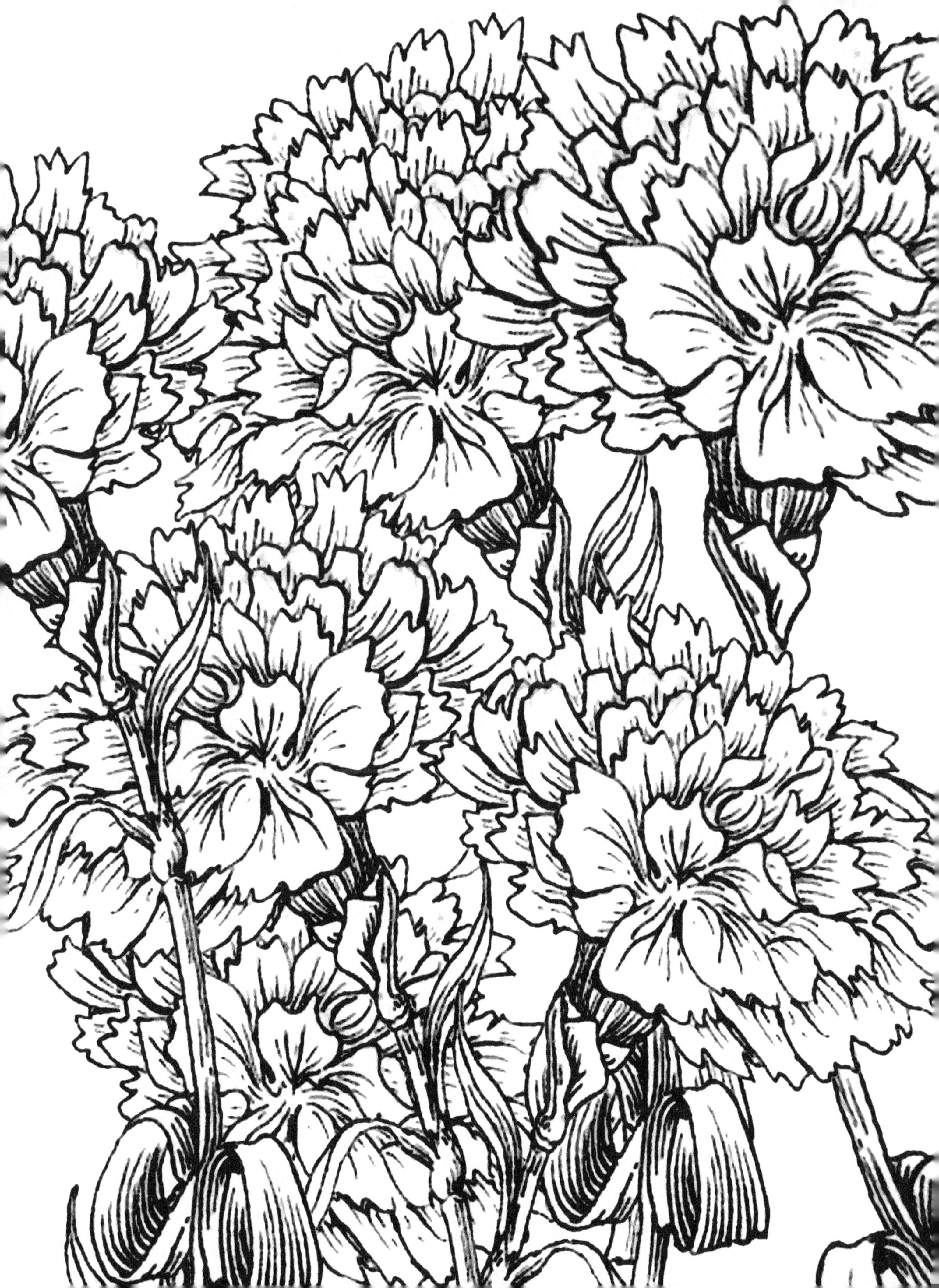

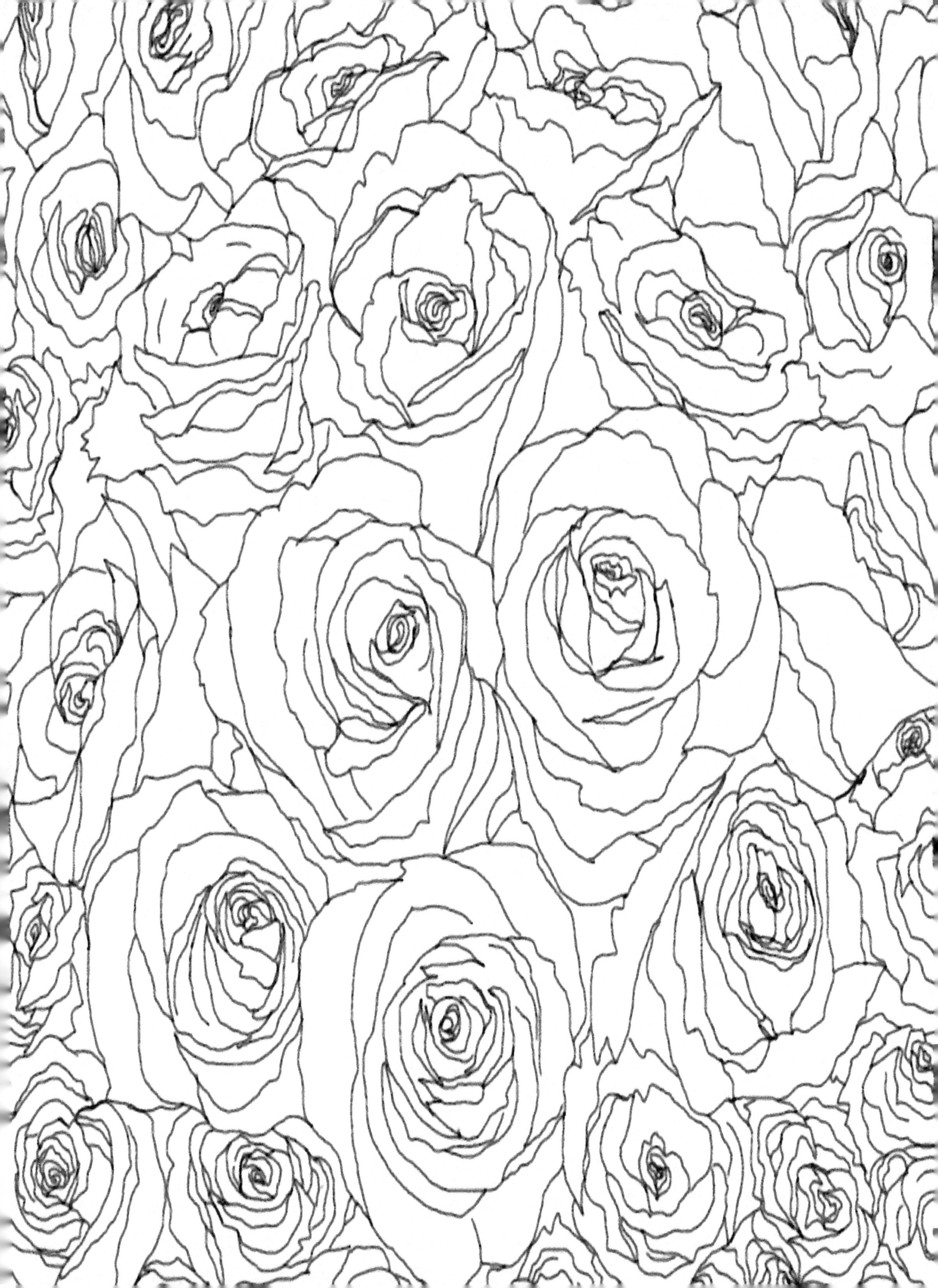

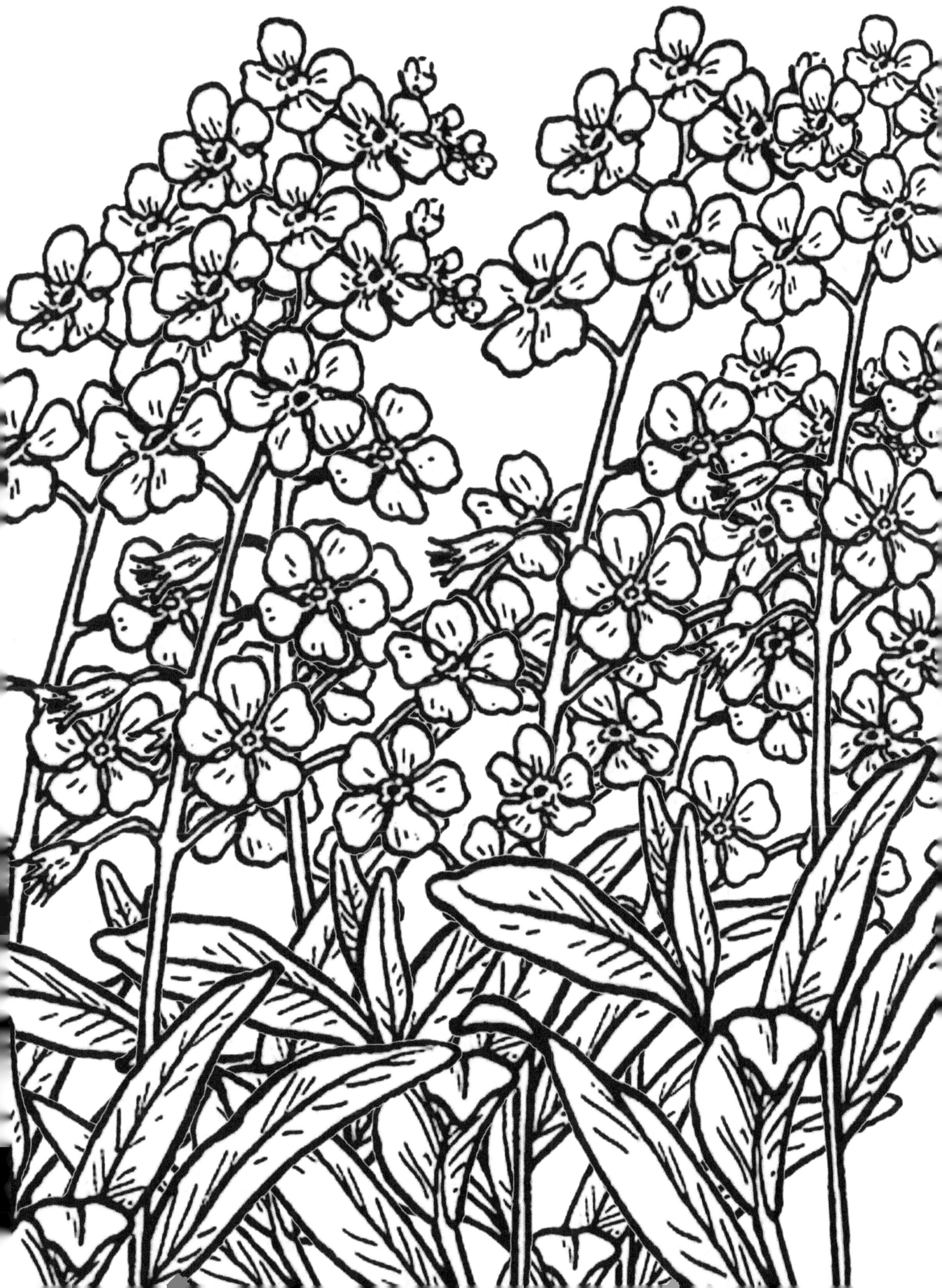

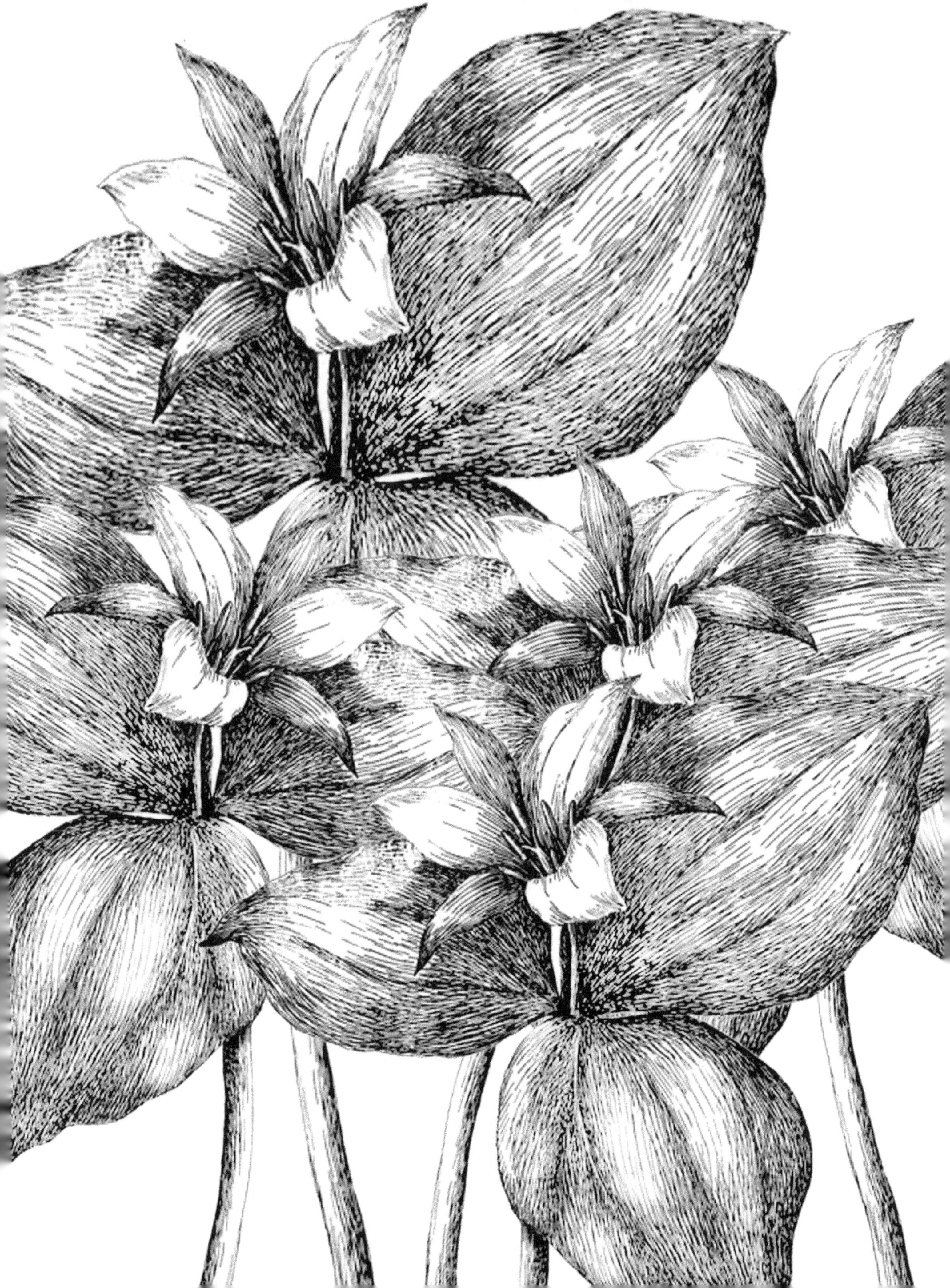

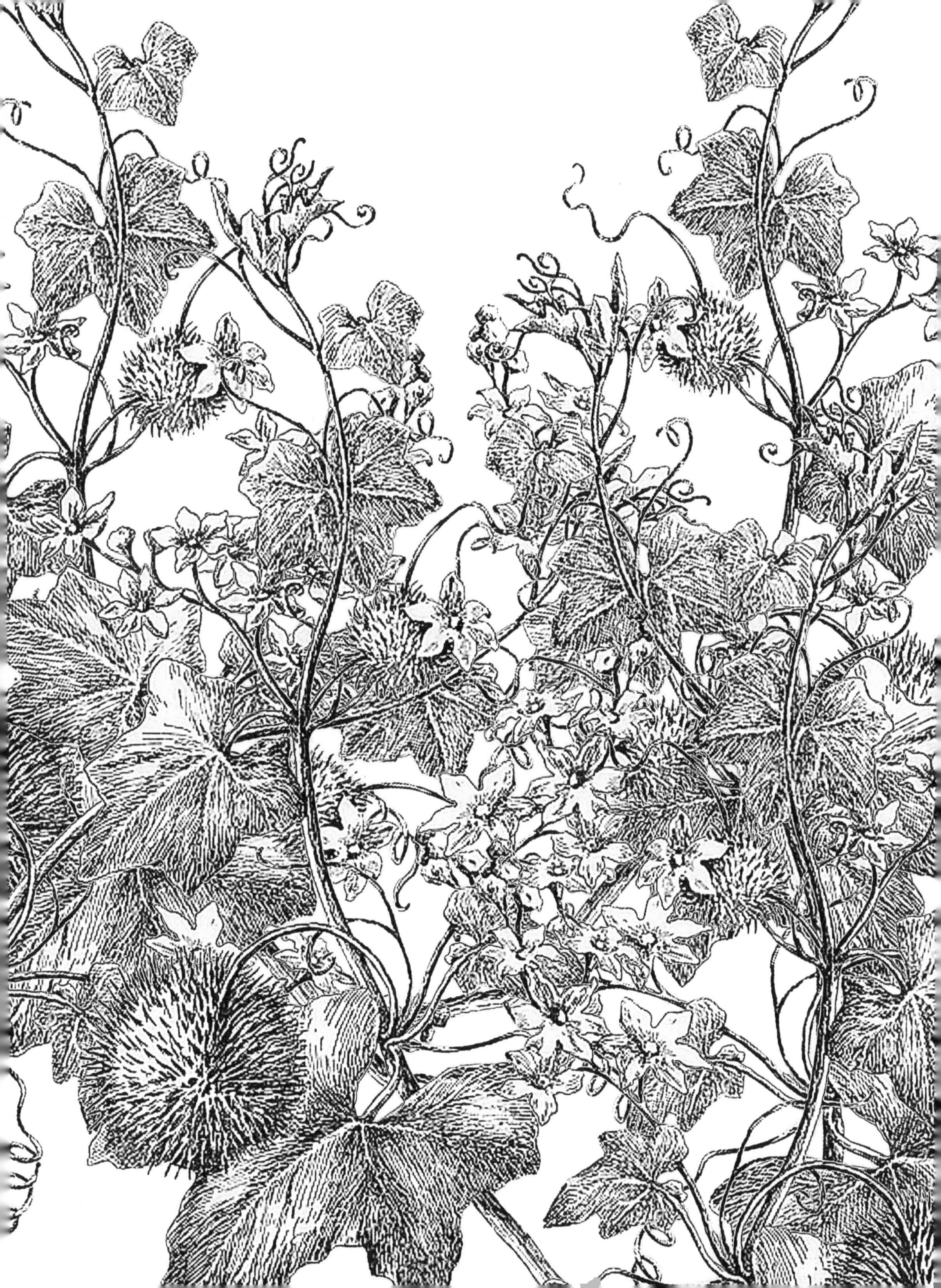

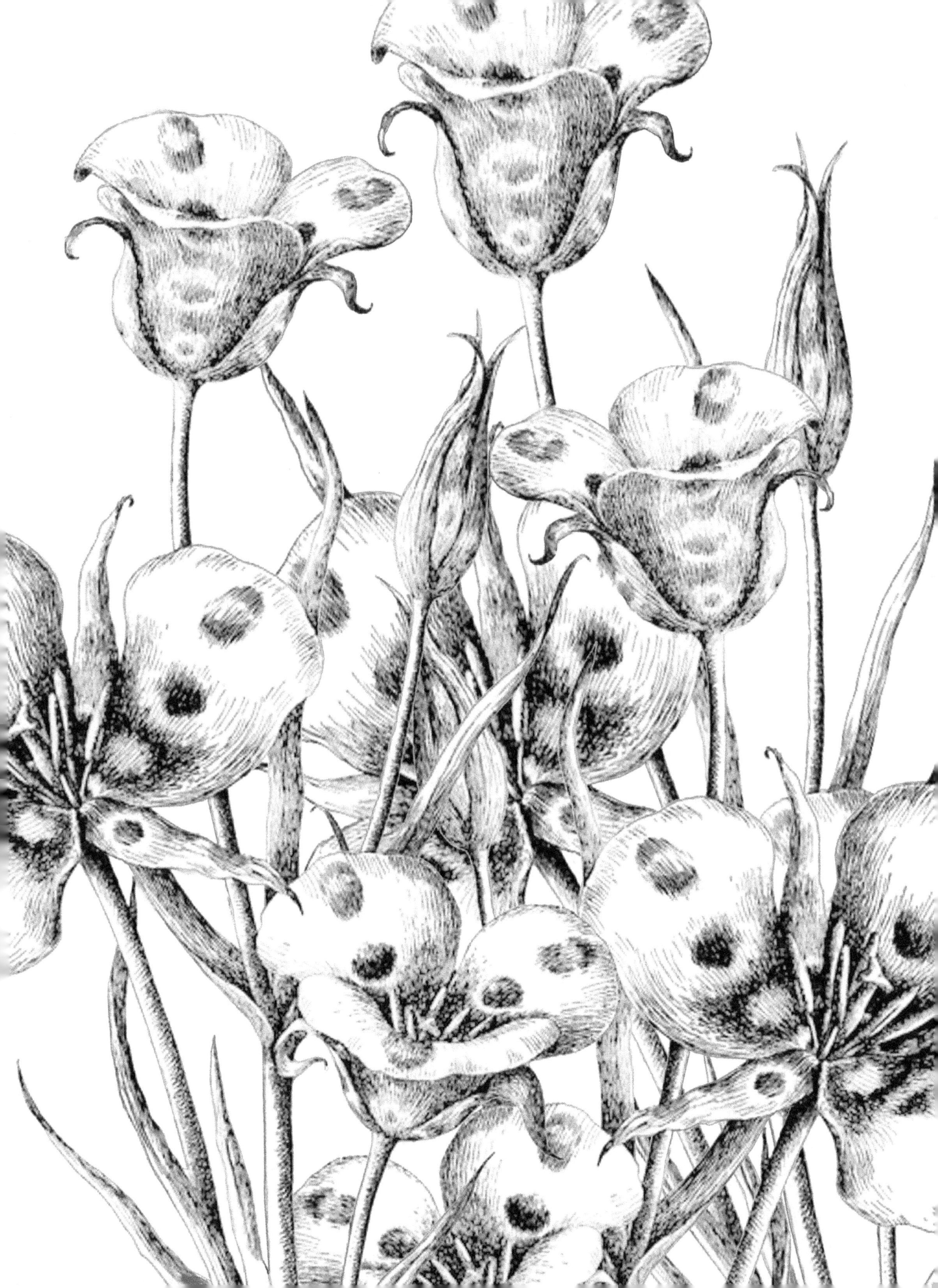

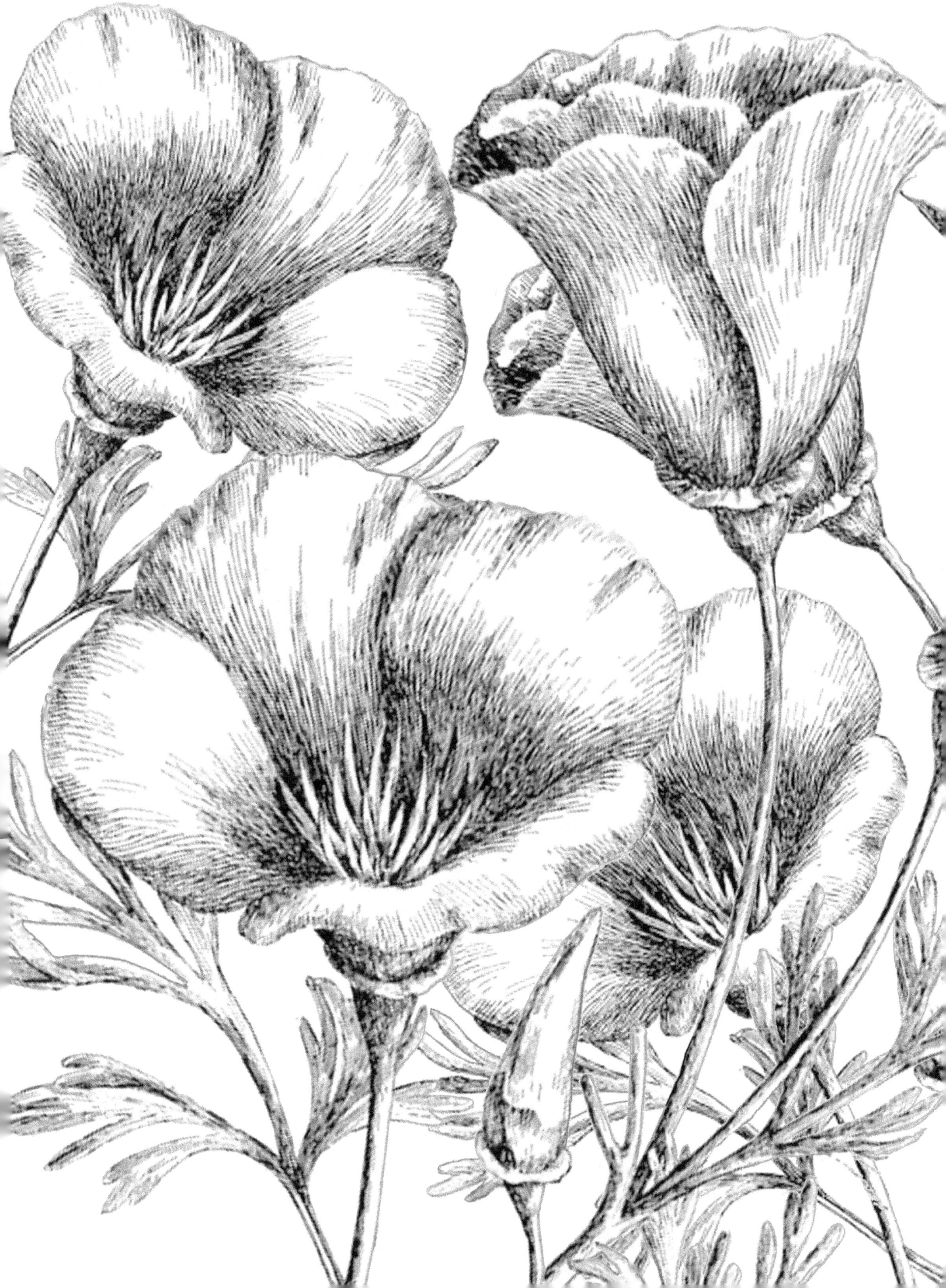

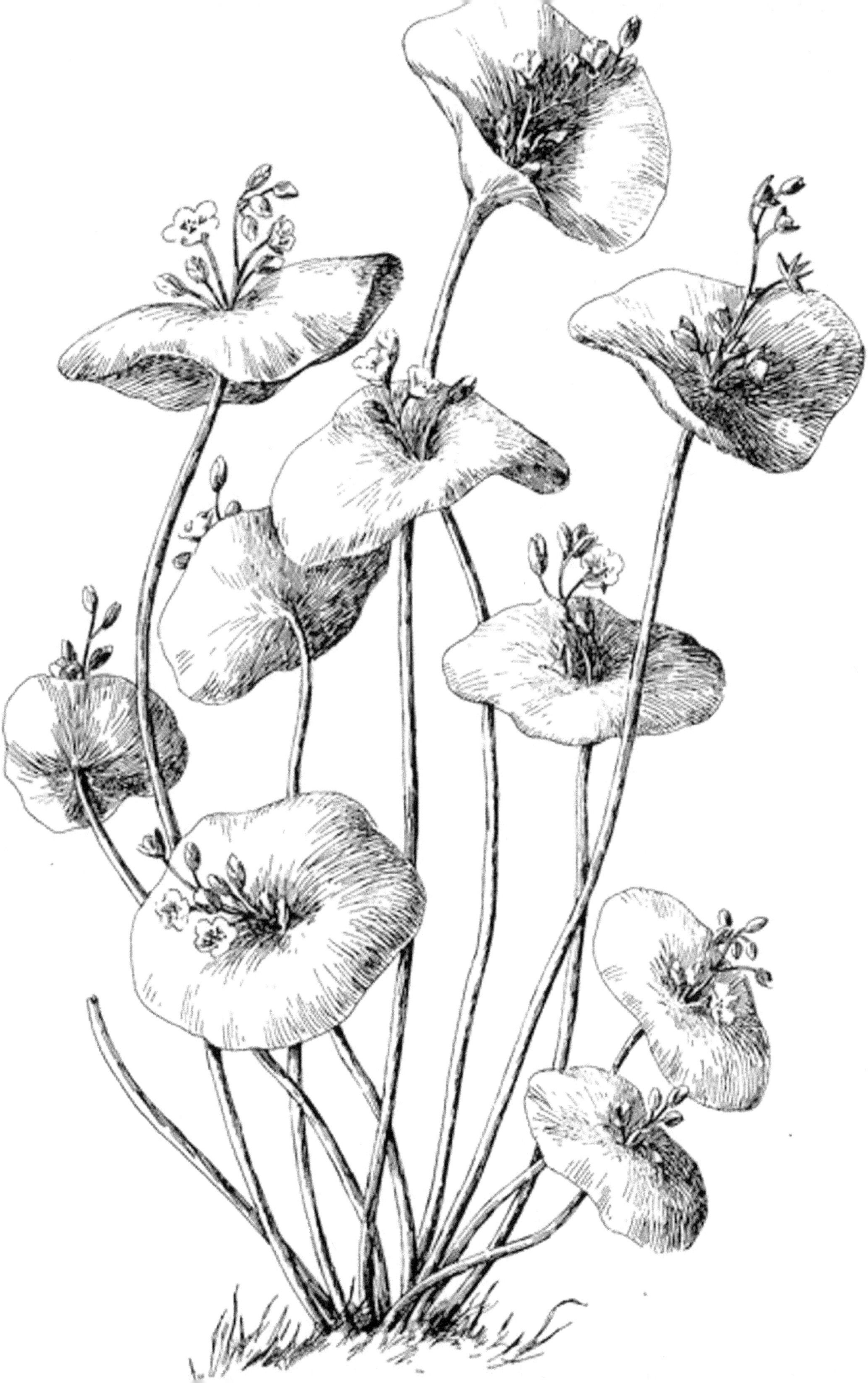

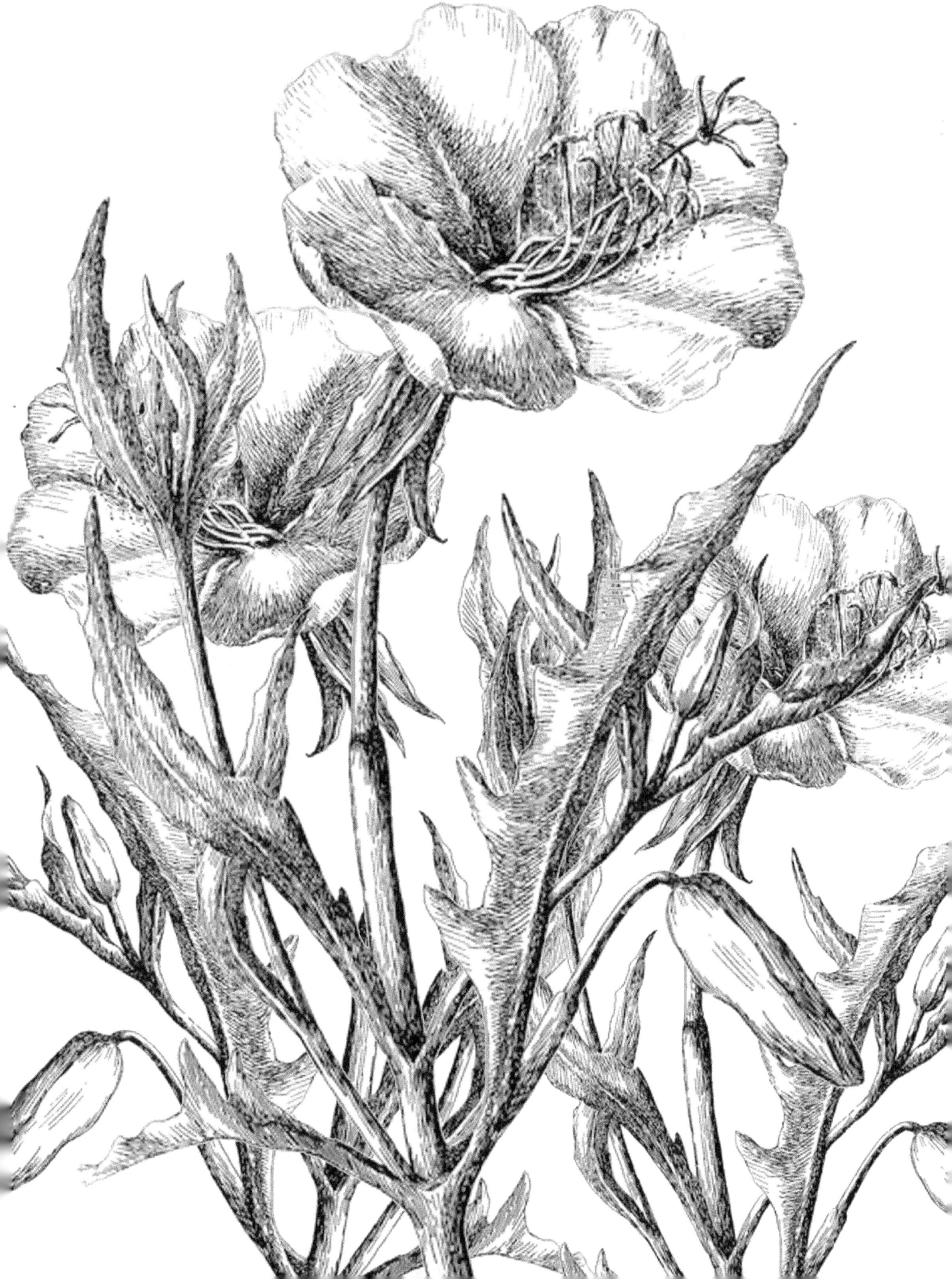

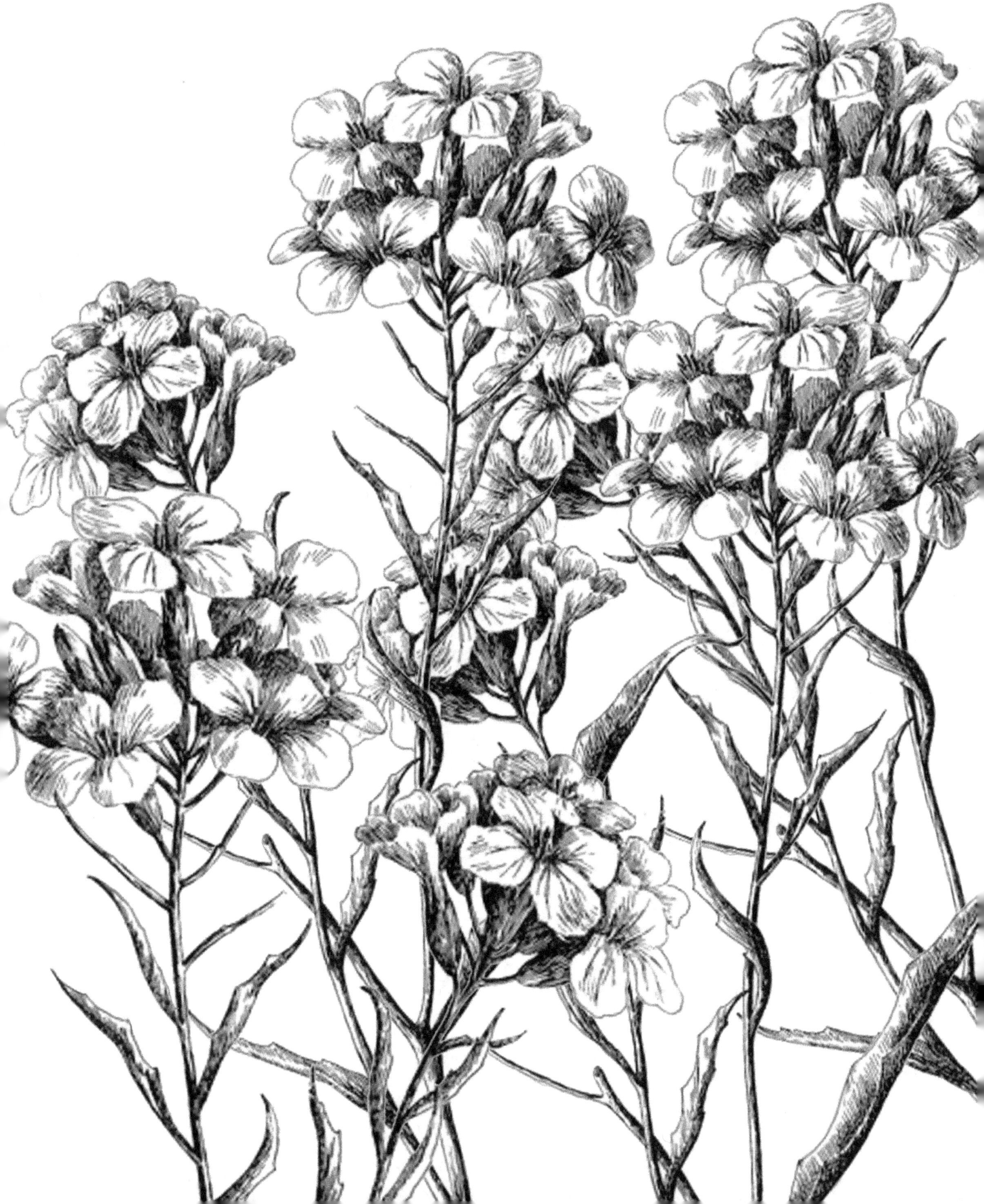

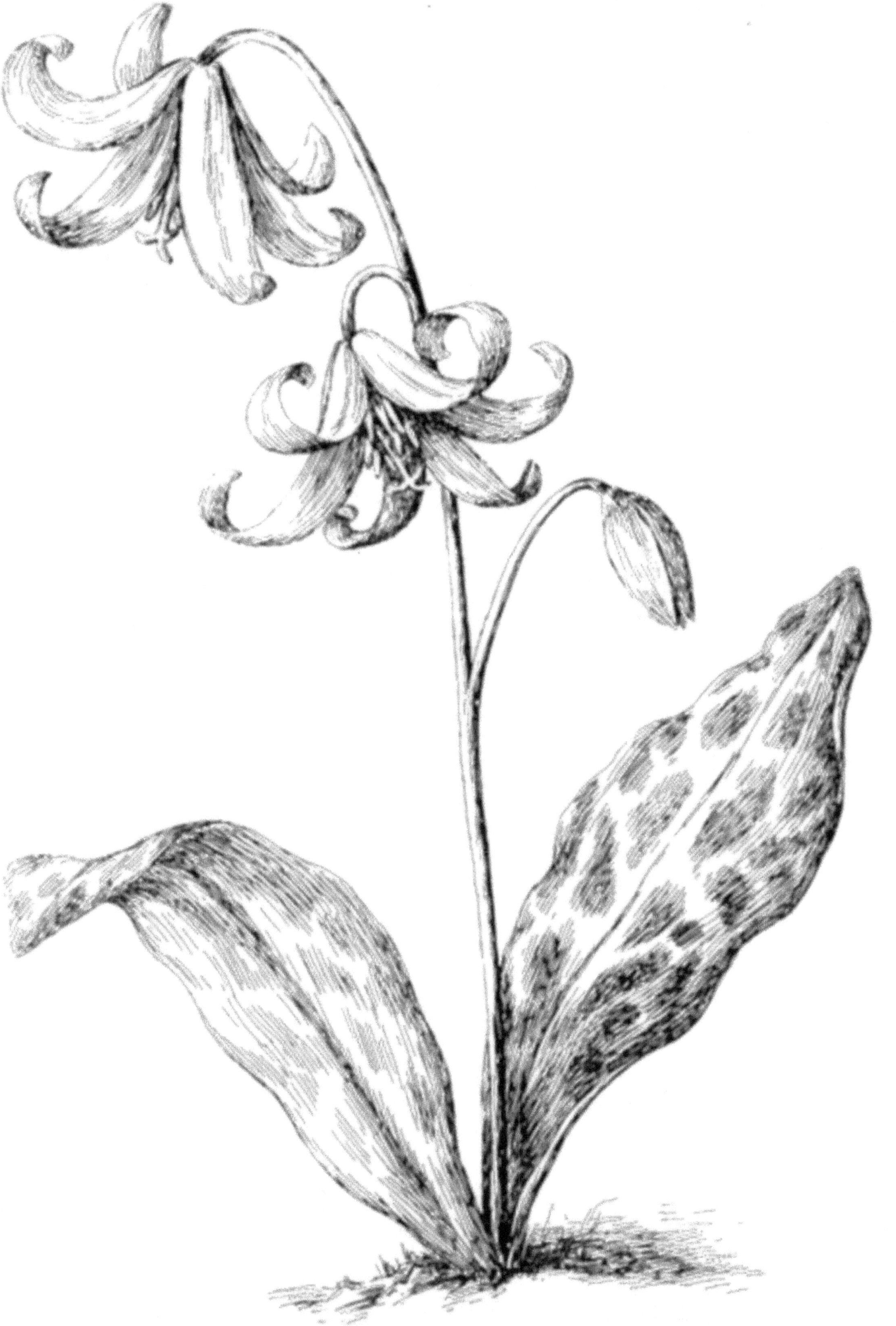

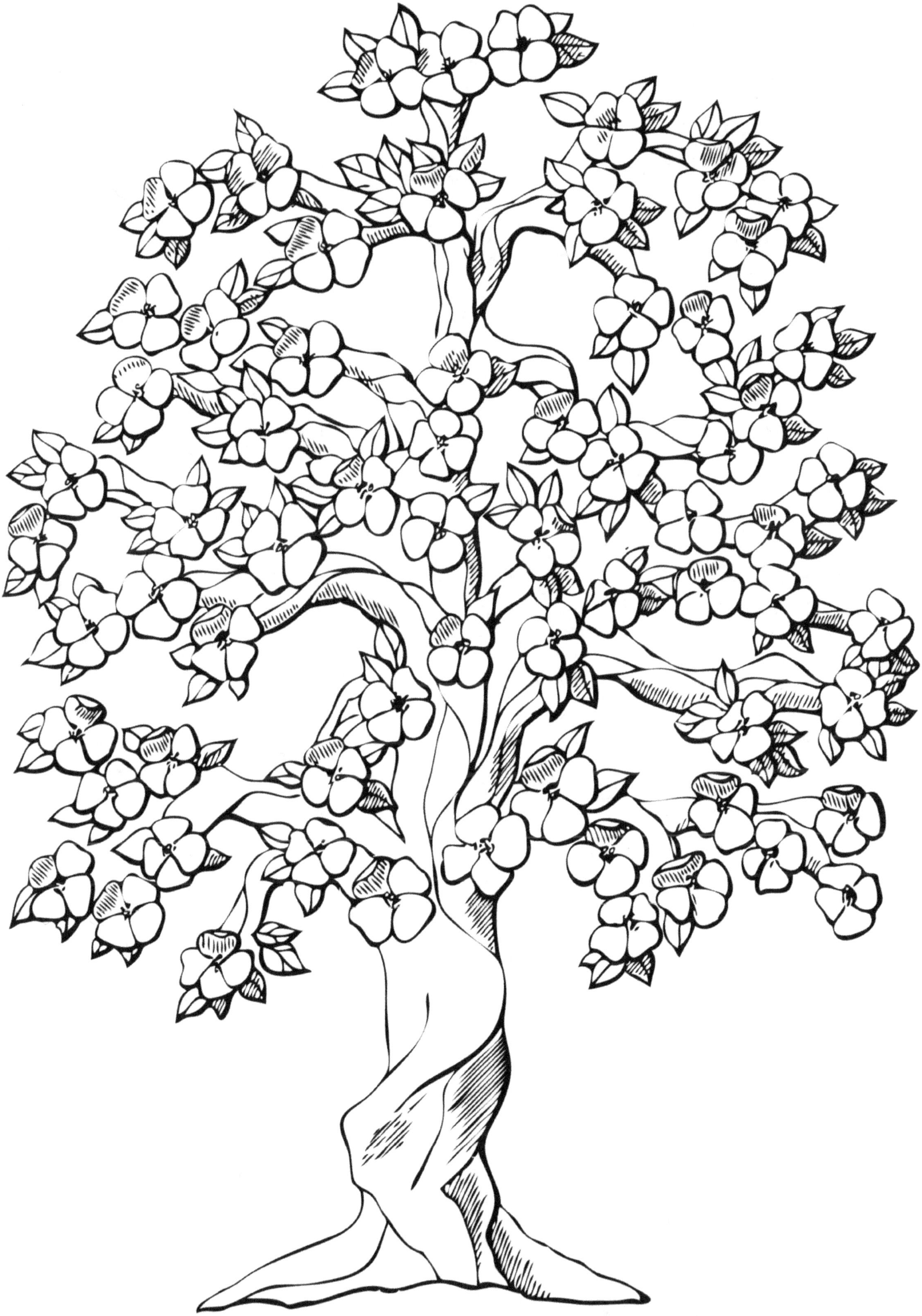

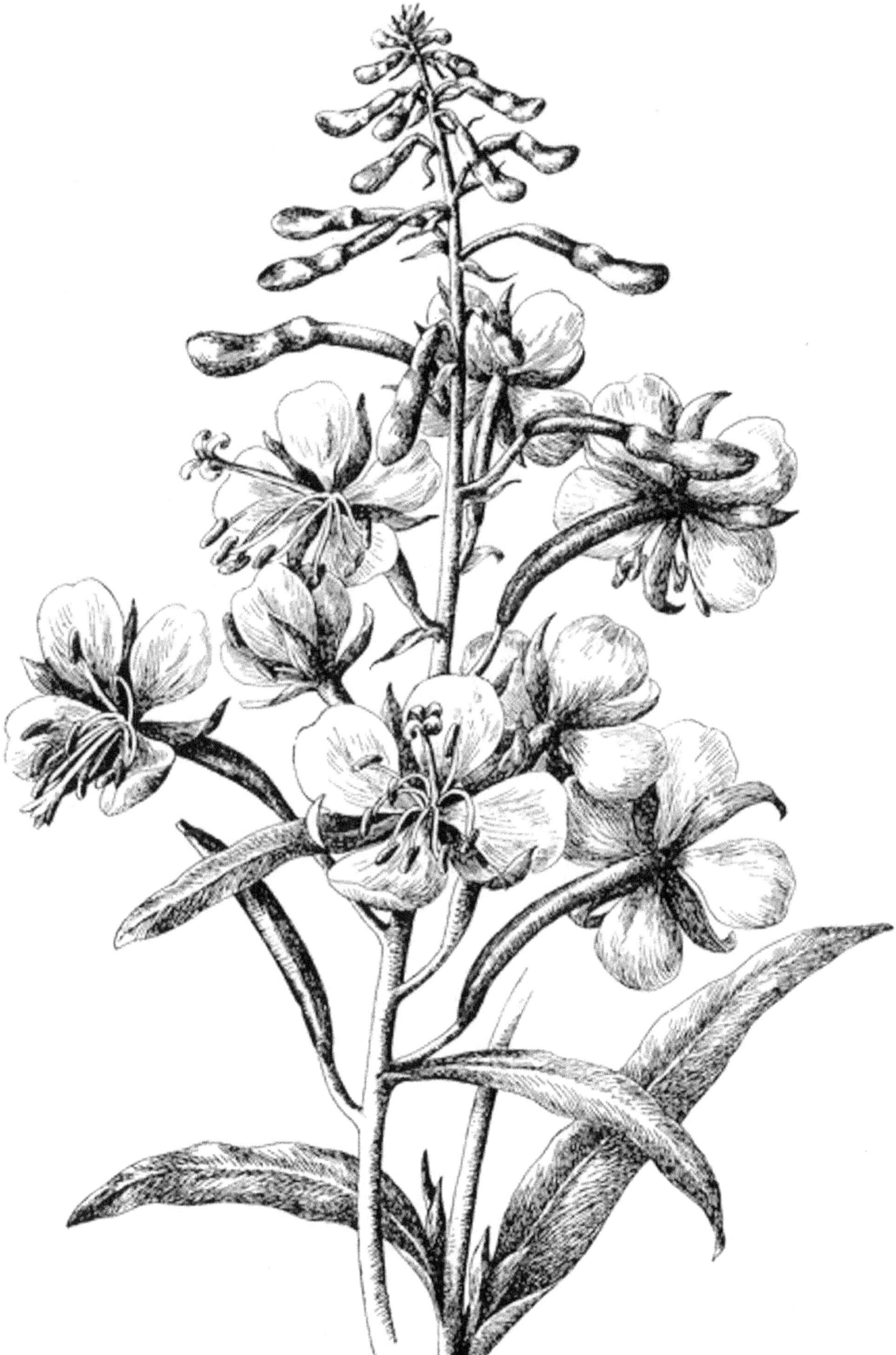

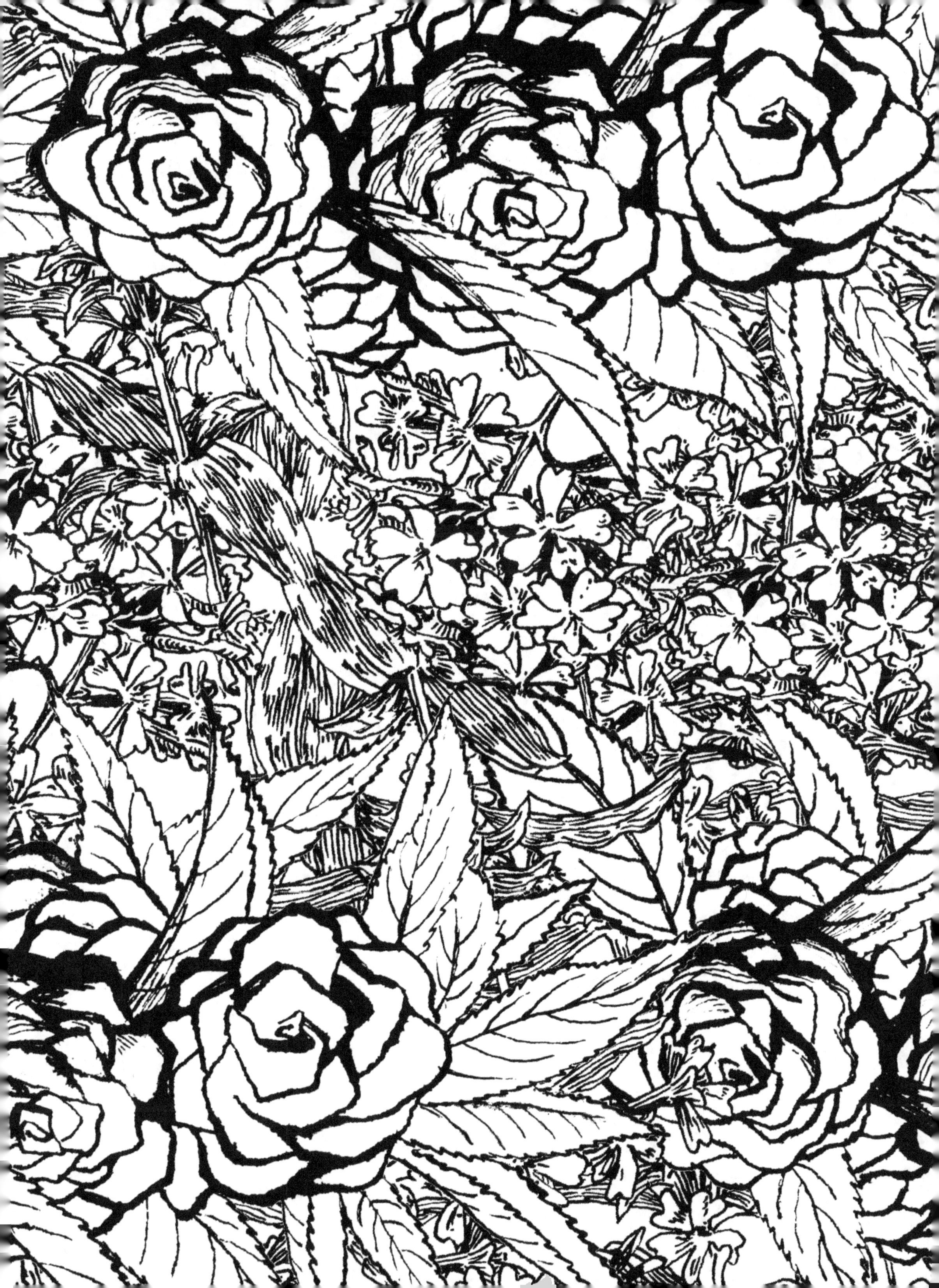

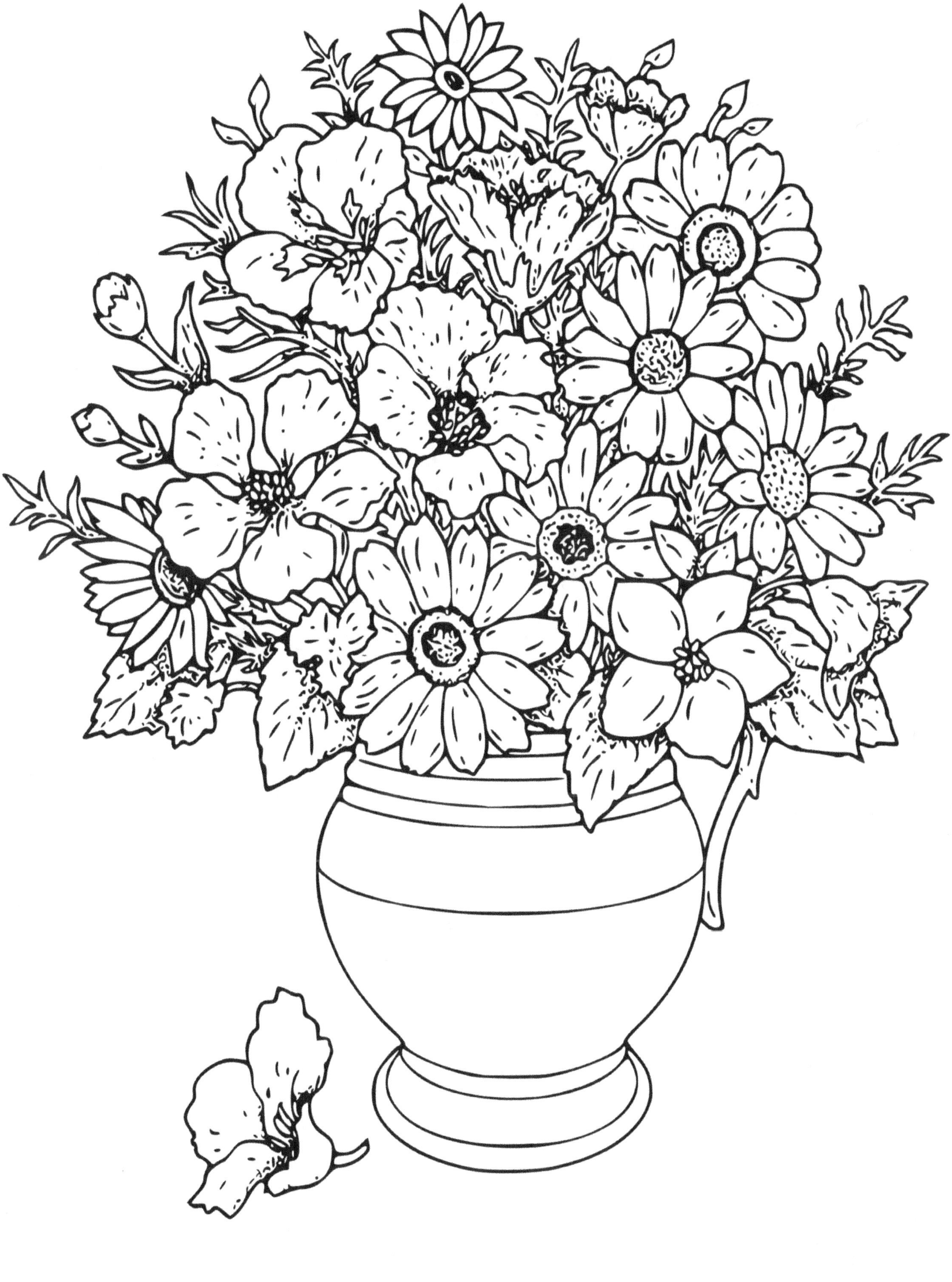

www.ingramcontent.com/pod-product-compliance
Lightning Source LLC
Chambersburg PA
CBHW080447290526
45791CB00008BA/2635